THE MOSTLY TRUE MEMOIRS OF A WITCH

"Mitchell King's remarkable first book is entirely his own, wild and adventurous, sexy and scandalous, abulous in almost every sense of the word. Like Scheherazade, he tells us, *I lie to keep my sisters alive*. His "sisters" are his generation of queer men born near the end of the AIDS crisis in this country, given medical protection but precious little in the way of culture or tradition – because, as King says in one of his characteristic tones, *dead/ daddies don't dance*. Operatic in its depth and intensity of feeling, restlessly energetic, never far from a raised eyebrow or a camp wisecrack, this book is a fierce, scary, passionate pleasure."

—Mark Doty

"Broken bodies, busted wigs, silver boots, grinding poverty, grinding, drag queens, hustlers, homophobia, the specter of HIV, the specter of a dead sister, of violence, of death by nightclub shooter: all of these are cast into the cauldron of *The Mostly True Memoirs of a Witch* to stir up its freshly improvised enchantments. The scene is a millennial dead-end, the hero is anti-, the bodies are everywhere, alive and dead. "I have known you through our frequent endings— the / unprotected kiss on my neck—the impossible about you," King's narrator says. But even as despair floods these poems, so does resilience and beauty and grace, for rising waters give us equal "chance at drowning / or salvation."

—Julie Sheehan, *Bar Book: Poems and Otherwise*

THE MOSTLY TRUE MEMOIRS OF A WITCH

poems by
Mitchell King

STUBBORN MULE PRESS

copyright 2020 Mitchell King
cover design: Elim J Sidus
interior art: Elim J Sidus (from design by Mitchell King)
ISBN: 978-1-950380-93-0
LLOC: 2020932186
Stubborn Mule Press
Devil's Elbow, MO
stubbornmulepress.com

Who says the absence of a witch
　　　　　　in-validates his spell?

—Emily Dickinson
Long Years Apart, *The Gorgeous Nothings*

Contents

The Ceremony of the Forbidden Fruit   9

Club Spells:
Orgy with Scorpio Constellation   13
The War on Witches   14
Fourth of July   15
Waiting for Our Nails to Dry   16
Michael   17
Hook-Up as Scheherazade   18
Lines from Poems I Refuse to Finish   19
Our Weapons Fell like Stars   20
When Does Captain America Arrive?   21
When Sylvia Plath was a Drag Queen   22
For My Roommate That Believes in Christ   24
Unlovely   25
U-Haul with Disco   26
Queer Fugue Diaspora   27

Spirit Visions:
Mad Boy's Guide to Astral Travel   31
Dead Girls   33
The Summer I Stole My Dead Sister's Ashes   35
Lullaby with No Money   36
Moontalk   37
Cowboy Fantasy   38
Star Fag's Lunar Rites   41
The Hurricane, My Mother Told Me   42
Sleeping with the Wolf Man   43

Baby Fat	44
Shape Shifter Dysphoria	46
Boy Stuff	48
Apocrypha	49
The Year I Ate the Moon	51
Letter	53
Séance in Drag	54

Gay Boy Armageddon:

On the Soul Arts	57
Our Oldest Father	59
For Johnathan on His Gay Wedding	61
Longest Night	63
Spirit World Death Drop	64
Trailer Park Warlock	65
Daddy Poem	66
Bad Magic	67
Here At The End, A Poem of Immense Gratitude	69
In the Desert, A Vision of Dolly Parton Appeared Before Me	70
In the Language of Angels, The Enochian Invocation of Gay Michael	71
Planet for Dreamers	77
Boy Lazarus vs. the God Machine	78

SECRET ENDING:

True Names Defeat Overdose	83

for mom

The Ceremony of the Forbidden Fruit

But to trespass upon that land is strictly
        forbidden—the magician lays nude

on his table—the sword in his hand was made ancient—
some things come into being without youth:
        Saturn and statues—these vanishing

interludes—we arrived late to the coronation
        and so the seats left to us were dinner trays
and singing cups—*a touch of wonder makes a party—*

we were told by law to be grateful that we lived at all ;
                and while the law spoke   I felt

the stolen fruit leaking sweet juices in my pocket
        guilty and precious tang on my finger:
        burst of citrus that I'll roll
my tongue around till hours later—the taste of gold I won't forget.

i: Club Spells

Orgy with Scorpio Constellation

The dead are buried beneath us and
I can read dick veins like a palm
        crossing streams like dowsing rods—

here our body is a cathedral—gold domed
and smooth, when we struggle
to wash the hymns of his

                        and his and his body out
                        the dead grind beneath us
                        to the music we play.

Dead daddies, dead daddies, dead
                        daddies can't dance—

these are not the last days of disco
or sleeveless shirts and thinking
        too much about loving love and running—
our future is as out as the dom-top in the corner—

it's all preordained: driver's gloves and tight pants
        —a tulip bending in the rain—

                        I pray for mystery when
                        he spanks our pink
                        and dead daddies get harder
                        than a bone in the grave.

Twenty five is dead year. I'm too old to be a twink.

        Some nights I pray *make me a constellation*

and daddies splatter our abdomen—like Orion—
bigger than this body and the time it must endure.

The War on Witches

—my grandma doesn't know. My grandma watches
the news. We hear a woof and I woof back—my grandma thinks
I'm dead//*talking like a dog*//coyote-hungry—I can't find any money so
      I work for it in the night.

My grandma thinks I'm a bad ghost walking into her house. I look like
cousin of a cousin from at least fifty years ago. I look like somebody
that used to cut her hair in the city. I look like my face is a vacant hole
where a shotgun could be. I don't know why I'm telling you this//*I've
never seen the news-clipping*//if you were going to kill me I'd be killed
      already. I'd be in the trunk or in the shower

or on the roadside with dirt and silver coins for eyes. But I'd be
surprised if you did it so peacefully. I'd be surprised if you didn't pray
to your crusader's cross right after//it's all such easy math anyway//
adding the weight of my heart as a mark of your purpose
      then the heft of that number

growing bigger and bigger—*my grandma doesn't trust strange men.*
      My grandma doesn't know what happened to her friends.

Fourth of July

America, this is this last poem where you love me.
Water balloons wet my white shirt, boys playing
in the neighborhood, waiting
for the explosions   and the glitter that comes after—
the *boom boom boom* as thunder in the heart.

For the one boy whose father is away from home I make
a garland of weeds and one bluebonnet—a gift of green and blue
on this rare night when the cicadas have more secrets than I do.

Of course I wanted him to love me. To play house where I was
his wife and he my salesman always leaving late for work—
the other boys would be our children

and keep me company while I worry about their father all day.
Has he eaten? Is he cheating? Are there pettier girls than me?
Do you see where this is going? This is the last poem where you
love me—before I tell you the truth—before the cicadas erupt
from their husks in laughter.

                    I place my garland on his head. I tell him
what he already knows about the heat, how our shirts are wet
from water balloons—how we should probably take them off. This
is the last poem where you love me and how I learn
to hate myself.

~~*Fucking Faggit.*~~

In my grandparents' backyard—*America!* you were the first boy
                              to turn my face away.

Waiting for Our Nails to Dry

We're flirty and broke—a lucky day is
when someone else pays for dinner. Leone brings

      home a bottle of stale champagne from the bar.
Everyone had a rough night—none of the tables tipped
as they should—it was thankless

service all over. We turn to beauty and the future. Again and
      again. Leone is moving to L.A.—or so she says—*this place
is dying*. We've got ghosts already, it's September and the dead are
a hobby we hang on the walls—the painted skulls and candy bones
that get stuck in our teeth. Paige cats over her nails

      waiting for them to dry so she might as well tells us about
Europe—her fabulous summer trip; the expressionless women
in beautiful hats—*we could all go!*—and I love a plan that won't
happen—it's a daydream in the evening as we listen to the last
cicadas rumble into a sudden
      hush   and each year we forget how quiet the world can
get. The neighbors hate the garden we don't have the hearts

      to tame; in a month we'll have to cut it down. Marie told us
that leaving wasn't an answer—*in a couple of years you'll just move
back here anyway*—the smell of new wood and rain all around us;
they're building condos down the street—an arsonist is our only
hope and we pray every night—*the rent keeps going up.* Kevin
shakes his umbrella. James might be coming into town

      and we're getting ready—*aren't we so intimate?*—we'll have
another old friend for a couple of days.

Michael

Michael crosses broadway and I'm not there—
in October it's impossible to avoid the rain the weeping

and not-yet-over-it month—the month of not-yet-over-*you*
thirty one days of walking around each other and I still hadn't
plugged in the space heater because I was afraid

it would catch the house on fire—afraid even if it would keep
us warm on our way home from the blood test where I learned
phantasmancy winking at the needle as it kissed the hinge of my
arm gulping the red

of my body like a soda: all sugar and good intentions—then
                                    the color of falling leaves.

Hook-Up as Scheherazade

my poor body double

left to her own devices—counting the black hair
on his forearm, counting the gray fuzz on his puppy-tongue—

    and pseudonym is a word that kisses itself in disguise

which is to say I lie my name into
    whoever you want, my husband, my king and slaughter

        he's complicit in the telling of these stories

touching me through
    his sheets, finer than my mother's house, softer than her
hospital lips—encouraging—how my first kiss was teeth and queer
angles, waking up with grass-stains and

        cricks in my neck—*a boy is an excuse*
        to linger in the mirror—
    an excuse to nail down the more nebulous parts
of history—my eyes are x and then y—for every man

    I am a different man   for every death a

a different spirit-at-war with her name: how
I found the well and filled it with water,

how I drank of it and became poisoned, let me tell him
how I found the cure in a land he has no crown over:
    a poem with no governor to demand tithe
        how I craved doom more than his future
    and the truth a man like him cannot know,

I lie to keep my sisters alive.

Lines from Poems I Refuse to Finish

I've bought another notebook   I won't fill   July
           was a month for dreaming

when I try to write
                    the poem   in which you die
                    I feel
                          as if I've
                                  killed you

the barn caught fire
            indigo snakes slithered out—like the hot
      purple
      fingertips of an extending palm   when I bring up my
                                              wrong doing—
I do not mention the devil
            although he craves the credit
for all my misdeeds like once
            there was a rich man, once I burned
    every spindle to neutralize an evil spell
    but the twelfth fairy,
who could not break the prophecy, said and *yet these lies shall tell the truth*—it is six winters cold in my heart
                        a girl gets eaten by a man

Our Weapons Fell Like Stars

        in the country of my father I learned how to build fences
between my body and all others as his fathers believed that a wall
was the only thing that would keep us safe while

the country of my mother held my lips as her mother before her
saw the future in a broken egg telling no one about the fist and

        the story of our borders—how a poem changes no
        one. When love came to my body he was not of
        this nation   and I left

        my hand too long above the stove turned
        red like the boy in another country
        where our weapons destroy his body

        and our own

will not kindle an aubade or a morning while
moons roll the map open and wane at how like a body it is

too small to carry all this pain.

When Does Captain America Arrive?

I have placed all my hopes with men in skin tight tights and fetish-
wear deflecting lasers and side eye, ignoring *who is this bitch?*
by brandishing the truth as a shield and a weapon of life against
insurgent

death—in the country where I come from everyone knows hate—
hate at a theatre, hate at a night club, hate at a mall; can his bicep
lift the weight of our pain?

I wait by the mirror and hold my head down—is this shame?
Hating others as I have hated myself, escaping to midnight fantasies
—wearing a latex cape and hood, saving the world with words

at night and walking, quietly, to work by day. His shield must be
like Achilles' covered in faces long dead and still fighting, circling a
perimeter of magic metal, avenging steel, bas-relief, a carved history
of war and the struggle against.

The wolves are paw-pacing beyond this base camp I have made
from news-scraps and artillery shells in a school long dead. I want to
throw down the walls of every city

that forbid us entry, or I want to colonize the moon, riding
Cap's shield like a rocket thrown out into the unclaimed
space between stars by a bicep that is a locomotive agent
for *Freedom!,* Wranglers and change like

a poem stronger than myself—that can stand on stanzas like sturdy
legs and redeem others as I have wanted to be redeemed in a place
between doom and Elysium: America as it could be—as a home for
all these hands

When Sylvia Plath was a Drag Queen

I have stolen a life. I wake up with the sun and put on her face—
the kids are away for the weekend and their father is my enemy
I write "I have exorcised him entirely" and then I kiss his picture

hatred has always been my muse—the lights and then the laughter
    remember the college bar they thought you were a peeper

for pissing in the stall when you were masquerading as ms gay
fraternity boy 2015 it was a hoot—for them and then the shadow

never leaves the floor
    someone you wanted and then something that gone

        straight men and beer-stink

    at once we want to be filled with them and be done with
        them befucked and befriended

and left alone forever—if Sylvia Plath was a drag queen
    would she have death-dropped into the oven? Would she

have filmed herself for hours lip-syncing her own verse? Shaping her
mouth to say "daddy daddy punish me im the worst" would she have
stuck a pale hand out for your spare dollar

    Would you give it to her? Would you pay her for her pain—

for the cost of the a-line dress, for the red silk, for the shoes her
feet are too big in—*drag queens don't make money*—but back to the
death   as that's all this exercise guarantees: an object to pray at
when it's all over:

Can I steal her death from her? And is that saving or damnation—my mother is smaller now than ever—her bones creaking with the cancer that hangs above us like a guillotine—

>the shadow is back and the shadow never left—it was dancing beside me the whole time /my leg in the air/ mirrored by the jigging tentacle on the floor.

For My Roommate that Believes in Christ

Oh Paul, the dog has locked himself in the bathroom
again and I lied when I said I was a dog
person. My rent will be late this month. On Sundays

> I'm not going to Mass at a church you haven't heard of,
> usually I'm stirring lettuce and bacon bits into tomato juice—
> three shots vodka— at a dive with friends that can't believe
> that you and I have made a go of it. Even

if it is built on lies, Paul, I do love you and your Easter
lilies filling the house fragrant with redemption and a promise
of an afterlife. I try not to ask whether grief brought you to the true

> cross, blood scented axis of resurrection, and I give you
> space when pray at the dinner table over corn muffins and
> grape juice—because you not drink—and you've never asked
> what I do at night when I fade

in well past midnight—full of tired glee. Perhaps you assume I've
returned from intensive and failing AA meetings. Or you consider it
some charitable act of god; that I minister to the broken

> hearted some gospel or another
> and perhaps, in my way, I do
> just that—like you I have hung all my weight on a thin thread
> of light— I too have wanted to hear God's belly laugh.

Unlovely

      there are many paths home and few of them are safe
in the literature of birds
      Death does not make them a good person—
      I have not misspoken
      Michael holds my hand but lets go—I tell him to—
at midnight I leave his house and vomit him in the parking lot:
in the literature of birds: there is a migration west of winter—and
Gays just want to have fun! In the parking lot I wonder if I've
stopped   looking   if I will and what happens after—
the moon's doomlight   sharpening—but not crescent, not quite.

U-Haul with Disco

between the records and turntable—rolling on the floor—here for the long good ride
chipping pieces on bumpier American roads
pull me continental and I leave a star dust trail from gas station

to gas station—urinal cakes turning into shimmery suds in the warm water of a body—*piss smoking like a fog machine.* Will we miss our old lives? The brick apartment. The old job. Will these new stages have an escape
hatch or

a tunnel? *If I knew how to disappear—we'd be gone already.* I'm using a pile of coats like a blanket. I'm waking up in someone else's winter and friends
are we not beautiful?
The strands from this fur coat—*opal liquefactions*—strutting in the truck bed//this is not the time for apologies//the leaving moment is leaving—I am either here
or I am there undulating with you on the highway—my head bobbing to a consistent bop. My favorite part of the song is the beginning. The unsure steps that first note makes. The slick snap of glow sticks breaking—
the neon future running down my arm.

Queer Fugue Diaspora

When mojo died
our clan learned the muggy mysteries
       of summer:

the suck of mosquito beside your lover's
       suckle and slumber—what was valuable but could not
       move was left in the hands of sacred-strangers to keep safe

with our dead along their roadsides   the pictures in a locket
              split between the silver boots
              they waltzed their lives in
                  like relics

on nouveau-saint's feet: glimmered pleather curving heavenward.

In these new houses you told me what I didn't know—*are you okay?*
       that I look sad when I'm thinking: I could hide this
forever if I really tried—then

you pay the rent and I know you stole the money—as winking
as a twinky body in this garden—Are we married now? Are we
newlywed—shot guns tattooed on our fingers we *bang bang* at every
minivan that passes //*I look toward the lens*//

       I am a thief of the heart

puff of blonde nothingness plucked
       from your clothes in the dryer
              and spun into something more useful (you-ful?)
       youthful and less terrible than that busted wig I wore
at first
and then never again.

ii: Spirit Visions

Mad Boy's Guide 2 Astral Travel

    Because the world of the soul has no objects, I took
    everything I would need into my body; on my bones
    I brought

the words that would bind you most like—*if you don't I'm telling mom!* I drank your favorite color and held the pink in me like a sickness ready for you to take it and all else within me away. Because you must have language to speak with the dead

    I learned: some boys can eat the moon//some boys
    survive on surviving alone//when I open my mouth//a
    year with no moon falls out—and I refuse to be
    understood

The psychic said that this place was without gravity
but I still walked with my third eye as a peeping searchlight
    in my heart   or on my forehead   or in
    the palms of my outstretched hands feeling and seeing
all at once as a monster in a fable that ate eyes to know the lairs

    of all other monsters—*make me an astronaut to navigate
    these stars*—because our people have no spirit guides

I came upon everything alone with my questions:
the spiral behind the milky way//the whale that
swallows light//an evil that has not yet chosen shape;
there is a ghost inside me waiting to touch something realer than
this body or the words that leave its mouth like a salvage

    and a dirge like when we die some things are certain,
    the artist that did not know us will convince others he did,
    the magazine will change

its cover from something red to something white—another dress
falling on the floor of the universe as unfriendly as goodbye,
there are voices in the poem that are not my own, and the time
that we did not remember, the time that we forgot
will come back for us with an obligation and a knife like you must
not be afraid to eat

    the bad thing's heart.

Dead Girls

> I wear my best tits and strut
> nearly tripping into the blinking streets; I don't want to
> talk to anyone

but my friends; I don't even hide it; the little knife I carry smaller
than a pen   but heavier with just-in-case-the-news-happens

just in case I'm not immortal; though I am powerful and bigger
than shame—*the earth is what we become*—I am not alone clacking

on these streets—*I don't want heroes anymore*—the gust of a
    folding fan

blows sweaty cologne in my direction, the door to the club opens
    and closes and opens again: one bomb can make
    a hundred heroes in an instant

> one disciple of the war god
> one misplaced look and panic—

the songs that come after rarely mention the dead: a new beat that
    we can dance to beneath the statue of the last American
    the red graffiti reads *Death To The Death Machines!*—
    and a boy

moves his hips like we could dance without these wars we wage
    with others and ourselves—spray paint in our hands—red
fingerprints on every future-tomb we touch and lean into. We live
    beside the dead and perhaps this is not the time

for peace and you have been right all along—that I count the
blossoms and ignore the blood pooling around the roots of my

favorite tree. The most popular song of the evening

is an epitaph. I climb into the arms of our decapitated
American—him missing some fingers and toes—dew his
muscles with swished up tears//*everything I do is like magic*//
opening my mouth

for the space where his voice should be; *when will victory
leave us alone in our beds?* The boy beneath the statue has
stopped dancing—his hips swung against a stone body, his
hips inviting all the hard love that a dead daddy can give—Spirit,

what is the difference between winning and losing? How
much blood is left for the altar—a funeral with tears still
hot to attend.

The Summer I Stole My Dead Sister's Ashes

The dead can see nothing that is shown to their remains.
    There are many waters both inside
    and out and each is a chance at drowning
or salvation. Some dreams pour through me like a night with no
    moon. Umbral and un-navigated. In parallel
    worlds you still live and throw your purse down
    angry because I left the party early because it meant so
    much for me to be there

and here you are under our grandmother's bed because
some nights I can hear her like she is sleeping under me and
    I don't believe in telling a body what a body knows at night
        like the night you drove the car under the over
        pass and told me
we should run away three weeks before you died.

The dead cannot hear our apologies about love or our wants
    and I've placed this poem all over trying to write the end
    with my body intact and yet why should I live while you
    do not?
The sun rises and hurts. This is not a poem about what comes
    before or after. The sun sets and hurts.

This is a poem about pouring everything out of the vessel
and hoping something might find a way back in.

Lullaby with No Money

Talk to yourself about work songs, although you have
no job, talk to Money like Money might be persuaded.
Wear a red tie to your meeting with Money.
In the mean-time interview the dead.
Ask the dead for money. Tell Money you love Money.
Dismiss

the dead. Be belligerent with Money. Since it's all imagined
anyway, be belligerent with boyfriend too. Tell boyfriend
to get used to your mother's cooking. Ask your boyfriend
for Money. Boyfriend says

No and isn't that just like him? Say *Well darling, what is loving
for?* Break up with boyfriend. Resume negotiations with Money.
No middleman, imagine *independently wealthy.* Money is
unmoved. Money recommends Chance. *Have you given the
lottery a try?*

Moontalk

Satan reads my poems in the dark,

my moontalk will resist translation; a haunted sprawl dotted
with dream-cities. I have a pink chest that an old boyfriend left
and in it I hid my hissing secrets: the snake   I failed
to mother, the omen of all my omens, the heart-stop
in my model-palm—the short curves of life line and wealth

        line wilting into shallow canyons, *a poet's hand!*, we laugh,
it's my first night in hell and I let him hand me more than I need
like sex is giving someone permission to destroy your
        feeling with a smile on their face—Satan moments tie me
back together—these proud beauticians threading terror and

moontalk is not for everyone; certainly not the Angels
who cannot keep count of the graces growing from their backs;
holy and unattended. They tell me *some of us are cursed with an
over-abundance of gifts* while I practice automagic writing—pencil
tip drifting like a planchette; I haven't heard a thing from her in
years. I can make a circle with two cute *x*'s for eyes. I can make a
mouth with no voice.

        ~~I heard voice is the first thing that memory forgets~~ but I
can't remember who told me that; how many dead are reaching
through some record? *When you don't know what to say; it's
okay to ask a question.*

Can you understand the milky gibberish of a pearl dropped
among the stars?—My moontalk makes no sense;
        this is not a new story—I've stopped sleeping
        with the door unlocked.

Cowboy Fantasy

James Dean

slides the rifle across his back and he looks just like
                 Jesus—fills the tv with his shoulders like
the sun—daring me to look at the long arms, the wrists
hanging limp   in the living room of my grandparents'
house—*now that's a cowboy*—and of course he was

all handsome and untame. Before I understood dying—*the
red metal dragging behind his blonde hair like a comet*—
or that's how I pictured it: gruesome and perfect.

//

body becoming a body
         myself gushing as an oil well.
I thought I invented it.   I sawed the handles off shovels
to dig into my darkness   for more darkness—
      when my father and his father went to dig,
rake leaves, hallow a shallow grave for the dead dog
      in the backyard

nothing could be gripped right. So I devoured like a farm
hand with my wrong mouth. So I learned
about splinters and Vaseline.

//

The night you talked about the boys you knew on
Christopher Street where he worked in a garden shop and
smelled like lavender

Or he only wore black jeans   even in the summer
and the moustache like a bridle and the one that grew

roses in his apartment but
the boys in your stories kept dying and

                        I wanted to be alive forever

//

When I tried to pierce his palms with my tongue—I said
that the rivers will outlast us

that I won't be a sunset or a moonrise that
the muddy and the clear waters will live
longer than my prayer and my want
to be like him.

//

No cowboy has ever gone out into space.
     Though the light of stars travel godyears
     to flash on his spurs and blind
the boy watching his swagger from a window in a small town

and all my fathers crossed the country
to pan for gold in California where no one ever dies

sending home wonders like turquoise and fool's gold
a sheriff's badge—some smoke.
I wear this badge with no authority.

                        I fill my lungs with clouds.

//

My thick-wristed beauty—
my cowboy with wranglers starched to stand without his legs

like they were haunted. Like they were sewn together with
the names of the dead. *Sometimes the dead are all that
keep us going.* There are voices in this poem

that are not my own.

Every cowboy has his dead

horse. Every cowboy, a dead lover, so my cowboy became
like paper—blonde hair like an apology

a sunrise behind his head in the small apartment
in my too large state. So he had a shoot-out.
                So now he's mine but mostly forgotten
                    like a shape of smoke in a cigarette ad—
                        oh hat-tipping silhouette—
Texas has killed everyone I ever loved—

                              the first fag I ever met.

Star Fag's Lunar Rites

The moon is a god with a turquoise beard.

        He texts *"u up?"* when he's
kept me awake—*the moon is a fuck-boi*—one
white eye pouring in my window, white eye
winking that I can't sleep. Sometimes the
moon is a stand in for love.

Sometimes the moon is a rock in the sky—
waiting to plummet above his temple where I
approach the altar and am made liquid

nosebleeds in the cold air—who doesn't like a
river of blood?
        Who is not envious of this orbit?
I wash my face in the porcelain basin and
outside the temple I have seen the doom you
are afraid of
and I tell you the moon is not afraid

to drop his body above mine and ensure
obliteration   *or love.*

The Hurricane, My Mother Told Me

About the sharks washing up in the garden; when she was a little girl
dragging them by the tail back into the water and the powers
that she knew; tooth-fairy and helpful

      mermaids with coral forks and coral knives—
the rabbits her father made into a stew;
the crying into a hot pot of boiling meat, the skin pulled off

in one movement like the frisk of a gentleman
      removing her coat—*she was so afraid of dancing*; that the spin
might steal her soul away or crack the dainty of her heel.

Sleeping With the Wolf Man

Isn't this wonderful? The dead month kicking a little back to life.
The want of a party creating a party. Miracles stacking on top of
each other: finding the pentagram in your hand, spilling wine
      in the shape of a hope—*oh infinite vessel*—leaving plum
splashes on the bathroom tile. When the psychic girl at the party
interpreted these portents—

she opened the mirror like she was getting a prescription—
      put on one clear glove and dyed her hair while the future
gathered around us like a plot or a punch line and we laughed
because I couldn't tell the difference between what is past and what
      isn't while the angel of the evening bang-banged on the
door—wings twisting

like the hands of a clock. Night inhales us as we walk into it—
      more thing than person and more phantasm anything—
darling hallucinations—sycamores glowing like a ghoul-scape
in the park's black night. Ask me why I'm crying   and I cackle
like a breaking stick.

Baby Fat

I am feeling very powerful today.
I found a blackthorn stick—I say
>   *I want a lover* and I get it. I say
>   *Summer Rain, Spike-The-Punch, a "Little Cocaine"*
>   and am bathed in it.

The universe is the most attentive dealer, you can have
anything if the hour is right—I open the book
and my eyes ghost-vacantly behind you. I think
>   *Goodness Is Imaginary.* I say *I Am So Full Of Love!*—
>   more crooked than rosy//every gay man thinks he's magic//

>   And I am no different—in a thousand year forest: I dare men
to love me from a distance//like a red dress//

>   I might go out at any minute
>   or burn the house down while we sleep in it.

>   My witch-finder, my basher with a blessed
>   bat—it's sick

>   I kind of love you.

>   You too wear black and walk alone at night.
>   You too wear a wide brimmed hat—*I'm sorry that I ate your
>   baby.* I'm sorry

I aroused you with the kill on my lips
like a glossy gob smack
>   and its sick, *really*, I love the way you prayed in the alley
>   to pin my handsome shadow in place—
>   *my immobilizing love!*—

I'm a visionary's vision—blurry beyond
the horizon of your reach
a realness without implications undeniable and
vanishing

Shape Shifter Dysphoria

—don't tell people how I'm doing 'cause
I don't wanna ruin their goodtime
      a goodtime is a goodthing not to ruin
right? Like the night at the party

(and all the time that shattered after) and I didn't say

i don't wanna be here (not the party—Here with the capital
Here like alive Here like the only place that death can happen
Here as in
      fuck this present moment)

and I know
and I know
and I know

not very much except that I should be grateful for everything
for sun and moon and especially when they pass one in front of
      the other like a pair of hands that will never touch—
imaginary handsome man isn't a faggot like me
      or he is me with another face and a better job with no
      anxieties about tomorrow—

and it's been days near this green water & so I've been dreaming
about a flood
      mythical & conquering

submerging the body & the body of the body—*the soulstate the
creep and stalker—*

sinking to the bottom walking to meet the fat catfish
the mythfish, nightblack, mouthblack like when you laugh

and open that tunnel between pinking motives   I fall into
        plummet and starfish bartering with the whalething

at the bottom of the lake—*i'm gonna cry, arent' i?* but I wanted to
take the stupid tumble in the waves head over heel *Oh*

        Licorice Night   I always wanted to be your wife

the *evil, evil, evil in Jesus Valley* as we approach

these cliffs—wearing sunglasses to look impenetrable around
your family because I'm stoned and you told me not to look of
earth and rubble & I've got a tree in my heart & its branches are
unavoidable

Body sink into the water
Body like a cold star
blue lips fishing for another drowning man
      but i don't think i love you anymore—confessing has
become a habit   blame the moon on my thoughtless
actions—I am wild and want you to be afraid of me.

Boy Stuff
the summer we found the dead dog

>pissing on everything/stealing lighters/touching snakes/not
>
>saying what we mean/ghost stories/wrestling/trying to bruise not meaning to go that far/purple/going further/
>
>blood/skipping stones/hearing *no*/doing it anyway/getting hurt/getting dirty/starting fires/*won't these burn?*/ singe
>
>finally/*sorry*/ but not
>meaning it/eating pizza/turning on the fan/going to sleep
>
>but not really/*you be the girl*/ spit/tight breaths/racecar sheets/breakfast with your parents/being polite/not saying a word/*if you tell anyone/ I'll say you're a liar/*
>
>*if you tell anyone*/bloody knuckles/beating a dead dog with sticks/stabbing the half-gone heart with knives/thirteen

APOCRYPHA

        jesus comes across the bodies

        they fold into a land bridge
limply

        kissing each other's bloat still
choking

  one eternal baptism   lung-
sacs full with birth-fluid

miracles and miracles and miracles and

        when jesus arrived he did that

  thing that jesus does where he
multiplies what has been given as if

scarcity existed only in our imagination
and isn't it funny

how we all know jesus's words but not

his voice? how *hello* could shatter an ear
drum—its throat bigger than a single year like
the precambrian is the earliest eon—

and yesterday is our most recent past and

    between these points jesus lifts a
sandal above the still water— the unmoving

swoosh of his socks

tilting heavenward like these many
whispered susurrations—
    these bodies wheezing

please give us rest

The Year I Ate the Moon

In our year without the moon no one went to bed on time,
beach houses walked a mile in from shore lifting

> their decks and porches as skirts afraid
>   of wood-rot and salt and fish-stink

clinging to the lumber. In this year I learned to see in the dark,
pupils going slit and slant like a poem or, yes, a cat

> roaming the alleys and making pacts with
>   night covered earth. In our year

without the moon every night was new-moon black and I stole
the hot water from your bath, the butter

> you left to be toast-soft by morning, I came
>   as a succubus and made your bed-pants

slurried with *come here and kiss me boy* dreams. I was mysterious
without the moon reporting my movement to the stars, playing

> telephone across the light years, *Did you
>   hear about our nephew? Get Calliope*

on the phone! Without the moon I lived in anonymity. Without
the moon I ruled the hunger fueled night with claws and

> sex apps selling men based on proximity. Without
>   the moon, I defaced all bathrooms with *call me, stud*

latrinalia—nothing tugging on my blood, bending the capillaries away
from my lips—in our moonless year, I went feral, frequently caught

        red handed in the only light of morning, alarmed
           by my need to bite and scratch.

Letter

Colin says I think everyone is you turning a corner.
        We walk through Westport and the terror shakes me
so bad I lay down in the middle of the road. *Get up.* Limp and as
paralyzed as the night I wasn't strong enough
        to break your fingers or kick you in the shin—the comical
        way I must of twisted; *handsome boy in a pretty dress—*

did you think that I would forget? I don't know if I really enjoy sex
        or if I'm faking it to seem cool; praying to black velvet
between my highs. If I could bring something back from a dream
        I would bring money because I'm not that creative and I
        have bills to pay and a body cannot be pulled from a dream
        as a body from water—

you get to a certain age and dreaming feels silly anyway; I was born
to play royalty in decline, the girl crying in an emerald dress—
        do you think this lipstick is permission? How it lines my lips
with their attention; like my mouth is rimmed with blinking eyes,
        like I'm a monster   for enjoying it.

Séance in Drag

Here is all the light in the world
traveling from my dress, godyears to your eyes, which are behind

        everything I've   tried to give a name to

in the kingdom of moths I wore white gloves so as not to disturb
the powder on their wings which,   having magic, allowed
them to fly around

    the street lamps which are less bright than

        pulling the moon down each night with a lullaby like

    you in the void and that red

    evening when we stole somebody's liquor and the hideout we
made running from the law

        with the branches around us like a secret
surrounds everything but is never touched like I want to tell you
about the night I ate all the cotton candy

    and kissed the boy with the boat how I fell in the water
and there was too much

    distance with no land and I hid my eyes in my powdered
fingers trying to muffle all the light I've gathered in the sky of this
dress   bedazzled by the distance

       that light travels between all these stars

iii: gay boy armageddon

On the Soul Arts

        The oldest temples were burning. In the
        white smoke like fog—memory
        was eradicated

but still, there was the problem of hunger, and now, without
memory, hunger whose name we had forgotten: yet we still ached
for   remedy. In dreams my green coat is leather
       and barely meets the top of these red boots you bought me—
    I'm in a box with a cord trying to call you: I'm in a box on
the side of the road and the box turns on its side//the box becomes
wooden: in the dream-that-might-be-prophecy
I'm in a box in the ground trying to reach you:
      the Friday after this, we crossed 18th and you didn't come back.

Wine bottle and purple splash against a window: this sound that
words cannot replicate: glass and body-break and the driver's voice
      insisting we were okay, for his sake.

        We were not chosen by prophecy: so
        dreams don't always pan-out. I am alive—
        but feel as though I am dead: this does
not remove the death from you. *Dreams can't wash that out*—you are
        truly dead—on Sunday I say your name in
        front of strangers.
    Wilting that they knew you   and I *know* you
but that does not make me know them: it feels weird to share you:
it is worse that you can be shared: counted out: measured: you
are now a finite amount

beginning and end. No new anything—I started slow—to make
new I tried using

drugs to talk to you: before that   prayer: and after drugs I tried both in combination: twice a day and then: thrice: smoke and kneel—

white smoke like a cathedral: my little pipe picking a new pope of nothing worth looting: who can absorb more misery?   No one
                                                                       and fire.

Our Oldest Father

had been a boar once and so, knowing a little
magic, I moved as we do in summer: all at once
            as air
that same instant in another place, *transparent throb,*
      the hot
beneath the moon as startling as the grip
            on your arm
at a party—there is no tomorrow yet
where we wear all our lifetimes
      in a single year: the strange graves that we've been under—
shadow that I join with
      ouroboros
               succ and succing: you are not my husband
                    I am not wife
though I work to delight you *wishes on command!*
blowjobs in the rear view—the dead only want a warm hand
         above the grave—the dead know too many years

w-2's hang on all the names they thought were
theirs: barista, teacher, handmaid, server then servitude
                            live to serve//serve to live

the poets cannot save us from consumption, lover,

      let me eat you before they can
      in the past
a man is walking across the battlefield draining semen from the
      dead asking us to reckon with his kind ugliness: *I do not
know that man*   love-hunter, he was afraid,   *killed in action*
a bad sign broke out   the redcaps   dipping their hats in blood
                            and so wounded

we bathed our bodies proud and broken hearted—
    combed the hair
        that thrilled my ache to touch
            because this is a poem
someone's soul must be burning

but you're so shy! Childhood and youth!
    Do not bring me to a hospital!
Another loss I cannot pay for so   I bend to you   cock-swain and eager: my own hardness in my mouth   you've tricked me,
    once again, into playing the forgiving part: pale   and submissive   and be-fagged in your bed.

For Johnathan on His Gay Wedding

Johnathan, I must   tell you
                         while I can
that you are marrying
the king of float trips and baseball our most American
American hero; he looks everywhere and sees Jesus

emerging from the water in slow motion: *droplets trickling down*
        those crucifixion abs! extending us scripture that I roll
into joints—*holy smokes!*—and it's true, especially tonight,
that nothing tastes better

than someone else's weed; the curtained alcove behind
the altar, sneaking puffs between vows   oh bride-groom!
                I am in love with fruitless endeavors,

I've waited patiently at the urinal and no
groomsmen have put a hand in my pocket—I borrowed
the bartender from another poem and he remembered

to bring a gift—*from both of us*; a shredded napkin
from the bar we lived in when we turned
                          twenty one—and we crooned
and our friends were too drunk to notice—I know it's not
appropriate—*these horns and this dark scepter*; I showed up late
       and uninvited
I've never been good at third impressions—and David

the city we met in is changing, on some street corners
I succumb to time entirely; the dreams of dead men and
       not yet alive men tell the same stories and not
all of them end with love. Now that it's over there are no
more secret

places to take us in; like when we built a fortress
around my bed and I stretched my left hand   across
    the width of that cold mattress and we were so still
like the night that we slept under was as fragile as a trust
that might   break.

Longest Night

Freedom for everything soft and pink!
I love how ugly I can be: there are three men in the woods
and they haven't started fucking
       yet—some of the sap stick sticks to their Calvins

matted in their leg hair, it hurts when the waistbands move
down legs—*just a little*—friction and minuscule hair pull

there are no curses left
       though I walk through the valley
             and the shadows
                   and death
my ghosts are with me—and *worried*— 'cause
I'm the dumb bitch that can't walk in her own suede shoes
crashes at the club, drunk cat in stilts,
       I say *this is the here I am from* first
before he discloses his hometown, sharing
a location without knowing
His name—at the bar we climb on too many surfaces
up and down, trying to give Him a better view, twisting ankles
in the name of fun then

drift downward in the mauve light   weightless and insufficient
      I love how ugly I can be
squeeze my hand and tell me you're not afraid. Squeeze my hand
      and tell me we'll wake up in the hotel room//by the
      water//salt sifting through

our open windows like snow.

Spirit World Death Drop

It's a wink, it's a shimmer, it's a fuck you
with a glance—*eleganza disaster*—honey it's my style

body drawling across the floor—taffeta ribbons streaming from my
heart— this is how *hi, y'all!* hangs in my mouth—a glimmered twang

in the too crowded club between ribs and when

the floor stops beating//the bouncer and I are the only ones left
dancing//stamps on my hand—so much red ink spilling over as
gayboy stigmata—gushing//*here is a mark to prove
 I loved others*//then no more ampersand or glister

    as sudden as the end of a poem

or a sister.

Trailer Park Warlock

In the story where we were both magicians
like the real kind, like the tarot—you folded paper into butterflies
and I caught everything on fire
like our friend's car or my bedroom or the funnel
of smoke in the bonfire pit—

I didn't mean to destroy the world

and perhaps you didn't mean to make it. In this story I name you
the villain and then feel bad—revise myself into wickedness like
everything I told you was a trap to witch you close.

I am not a good person. I hope bad things into happening—

you loving me in my real body: a man in the woods with a wand

                                                and no wig.

In this story love is not possible

like when you wrapped
your belt around me and knew
I wouldn't die—a mark appeared in my magic mirror—purple rope
across my neck; a sorcery of one heart wrecking another
and I was glad

to have it on me like a brand.

Daddy Poem

Daddy, are you not a god? Your bed
is wider than my country, forgive me these infinite
trespasses: I could not afford to tip the bartender, when he wasn't
looking I stole someone's drink—daddy, I haven't slept in a week.
     This bulging in my body has become a snake hear

the wonder working in my voice when
I say your names: John, Noah, Daniel, Joseph—daddy, I arrived
in the wasteland of your arms hungry as a bruise
for more color—am I too old to be your boy? I was a childlike
     when you opened me like a prayer—full of gratefulness—
                                                 praise

wide and empty enough to catch your changing gravity in
a net. Daddy, did I kill you with my want—? I kneel and
ask for safety when I leave my room each night; like is
that another death in your pocket or are you just happy
to see me alive?
     Daddy, I am not ready to die.

BADMAGIC

I have sent my spirit out of my body and stood in the corner of
every room. I confess have seen a snake eating its own tail
and

I confess I have spoken to the moon like a mother
    and

I confess that they deserved the justice
of my pricked fingers sewing the lids of white dolls shut with thick
cord and dull thread—needle bleeding my pink skin—and

> I caused the wind to ruin your hair before a picture and I
> nursed   the barking dog and the
> dreams you had as a deer pursued by hunters.

I am guilty of the tempest that broke the chimney on your beige
house—the bricks cascading like cheap comets—flammable as my
body and

> I confess that the brightness of lightning was my only light
> for many years while I lived in the umbra of your love.

I confess I ate the heart of a pig in a nice restaurant—
    and stabbed a pig's heart singing the names of my assailants
to the waiter while he spilled water on the table and of course

I made him do it with these charms the devil taught me like how
to carve stilettos from red coals and how to spin black clothes on
my nude body. I confess

I do not regret his barren fields or the dead cows or the soured
milk. I confess that I bought these from the grocery store so that
he could not buy more and
when I cursed him my tongue split like a pair of dancing legs.

I'm the most powerful witch you know

I confess
if I had kept my legs closed this would not have happened.
    I confess that the devil and the moon are my mothers—

that the devil and the moon are in love
and with their love I have crossed the sky heartbroken
    and clumsy as a toddler.

I confess my steps have trembled above your gables.
    When they found my sister's body she was naked.
    I confess I laid my body above these graves—I confess

I was alone when I listened to her whispers.

Here At The End, A Poem of Immense Gratitude

I didn't know it would be the last time we dined together—
Kevin and Julia were—predictably—late but brought kisses
and sorry's   *we couldn't find the wine we wanted* and since
      it wasn't anything the stove top couldn't fix with her red
coils it wasn't anything at all except an excuse to stay longer,
chatting now in the kitchen under the ugly lights swinging like
      an interrogation and we made our interrogations to each-
other, poking Caroline about a new boyfriend that we shouldn't
discuss but we all did *he must be handsome to make a girl blush
that much*

> and we had not learned the danger of words like love
> or separation

> and we had not learned how to spot a lie circled
> by the truth

and Andy brought along a new guy he'd been seeing for a couple
of weeks and we kept grabbing each other in the hallway—
      what's his name again?—and of course none of us meant
to be hurtful but of course Mac or Marcus or Mark took offense
and it felt good to laugh on the porch about it and it felt good
      to feel bad about it too and after we had finished the wine
it felt good to watch the candlelight tilt and waver like a dancer
in some faraway sky—invincible flickering—but
you might not remember how cloudlessly the sun set
how the night slipped in like a flock of black birds—
      poets are mostly liars anyway—how we fabricate a feeling
like tenderness and it becomes

too real to kill.

In the Desert, a Vision of Dolly Parton Appeared Before Me

Sugar—don't worry about what you're doing.
A poem is a zinger, a stab
wound, a band aid and each morning we wake up writing, hoping
to find that, yes, there is still more to love—

even in this mud season. Grab life by the rhinestones

read the signs—*dangerous curves ahead*—but you know what
you're doing.

There is always more to love—blue smoke on the mountains
wet earth under your heel, the All Mighty, *lipstick and wigs!*

Risk looking cheap, then go
and kiss, and smooch them boys in too tight jeans and, *Darling,*
      maybe pray a little too.

In the Language of Angels or the Enochian Invocation of Gay-Michael

My angel of Awesome Violence
en aaan de samevelaji maelpereji

whose name is revealed later
saba dooain i dulga capimali

be friendly to my shattered longing
zodereje adagita en mononusa
I climbed through the earth
ol torzu voresa de a causga
Pock-marked as the moon
├───────────┤ *ta a geraa*

To float in the darkness   after making
adagita ├───┤ *a a oresa* ├───┤ *eolis*
Pale Beside Your Golden Sex
├───────┤ *zomdv* ├───────┤
Silent near your holy thrones
├────────────────┤ *zomdv ne emetgis*

As your god is twelve kingdoms
ta zomdv elo i os adohi
Outside of time—   Chapel-bodied-Michael
├─────┤ *de acocasahe*— [*these words do not exist in your language*]

My angel of supreme love

           en aaan de iaida ├───┤
           The devil has set his fathers
           before me
           a babalonu congamplgh ├───┤

                     otahil totza ⊢——⊣ *apeta* ⊢———⊣
and says that I am the vessel of their evil:
od ⊢——⊣ *ar ol zir a zizop* ⊢———⊣

                guide these roads my returning
                ⊢————————————————⊣

                groove must take
                ⊢——————————⊣

                my venus-apogee
                en haniel comselahe
                the star that returns from the land of the dead
                en olapireta ar ⊢——⊣⊢——⊣ *a aala de a gah*

                I shall fear no father
                ol ⊢——⊣ *hoxmarch ag* ⊢———⊣
                Your hair and your forearms encircle Me
                zomdv ⊢——⊣ *od zomdv* ⊢——⊣ *comselahe* ⊢—⊣
                //

Five thunders accompanied your messages
⊢——⊣ *conusala* ⊢————⊣ *zomdv bial*

My phone nearly vibrating off the night stand
⊢———————————————⊣ *a dosig biab*

Holy nudes traveling along the aethyr's coil
En ⊢———————————⊣ *aethyr* ⊢——⊣

straight from five miles away—
⊢——————————————⊣

              Handsomest, I have adorned myself
              turbz el ol zir a

              In such apparel: mesh and golden rings
              ⊢——————————⊣ *audacal od* ⊢———⊣

In this heaven of expanding roses
a madariatza de ⊢————⊣ ⊢⊣ ⊢—⊣

        Feed me with your heart
        ⊢————⊣ *erm zomdv mononusa*

                          //

A Queer Psalm from the Palace Garden:
                [*these words do not exist*]
I stood against the slender cedar while you aimed
                The smooth whoosh of arrow-death

            Inches above my brain

            And the apple of knowledge—which you
                had placed there—

Split: one half tumbling into my left hand
            the other still suckered to the shaft.

                          //

In This Time Of Night
a oi acocasahe de dosig
I am your vessel first, above all
ol zir zomdv zizop el calz tol
The true dwelling
a ho fargt

The mobile abode of the spirit
a ⊢————⊣ *cafafame de a congamphlgh*

            Servant of the God Of Justice
            noco de a elo de balata
            The Chamber of Your Transparent Law

A ┠━━┨ *de zomdz* ┠━━━━┨ *vaoan*

But I am a relapsing devotional
┠━━━━━━━━━━━━━━┨
But I am an empty room
caripe ol zir a affa coredazodizoda

>Your wings are seven flaming wheels
>*zomdv upaah biab* ┠━━┨ *maelpereji comselahes*
>Dividing aeons : the first ritual I endured
>┠━━━┨ *acocasahe : a el* ┠━━━━━━┨

The salt-sweet taste   lingering
┠━━━━━━┨ ┠━━┨

>In the halls of that flame-bright colossus
>*a a* ┠━┨ *de ar ialapereji* ┠━━━━━┨

Freedom
┠━━━━┨
    Freedom
    ┠━━━┨
        Freedom
        ┠━━━┨
            In this art
            a oi ┠━┨

      //

You are the Truth of the Law

    Another proverb and
[*these words do not exist*] you say Truth and the Law
are the same god

      But I tell you the truth and you say I am breaking

                              your godhead

the bar tender runs a rag around his this rim   keeps a perfect
circle between his thumb and bone finger and

are these not Saturn's rings?
The death angel disguised as a good time!
          my illicit spectra: in the future there are no curses
          left to hide from—
can I get a ride with you?

                                                            //

On the way home and all the
├────────┤ *cafafame tol a*
Gay Saints appeared
ascha gah ├────────┤
          hovered around the car and
          ├────────────────┤

it was a nameless road that we were lost on
the road was lined by dark-trees
├──────────────────────────────────┤
├────────────────────────┤
They told us the songs of their dead legions
par ├────┤ *ome a he de a gah*

gay ghosts walking out of the woods
and I started to feel all disco-sick
ascha gah ├────┤ *voresa de a* ├────┤
[*these words do not exist*]

One dead name after another
the road moved beneath us like a serpent
el gah dooain [   ]
[   ] *orocaha aziazor a zodumebi*

Like we were telling unwelcome
stories upon her venomous scales
[   ]
[   ]

The dead speaking as a chorus
kept naming:
a ascha gah camliatza [   ]
[   ]

                                    Holy One, you must listen,
                                    En El, [*these words*   ]
                                    My Love was braver than my fear

Planet for Dreamers

Here in the poem you asked me to stop writing
it's a technicolored wonderland: every lane, a tunnel of love

neon tubes and neon turtles and neon
emergency exit signs—dangerous spaces lit up with electricity

safely generated off site. *Everything opens here.*

And where we are isn't really a star
as much as an imaginary planet and everyone assumes
Venus when they read the postcards anyway

and because I needed a location—*because I love you*—for your
hands, grease-wise and elegant, wide-palmed sleeping in late like
my father's and earth just seemed too boring.

I needed a bright sphere of phosphorescence
the kind of groundless beautiful that I cannot hope to survive.

Magical Boy Lazarus Vs. the God Machine

Stranger, I know you!
I twinked around the night-o-sphere with more
and more friends walking through the door—a curvature of bodies
like in science fiction the clouds are mysterious hydrogen and the
not-so-polite children of war heroes bash the heads of conquered
> babies against a sacred pillar—*Achilles, the armor on your
> ghost is tremored by our son.*

War is the always enemy of the future. The plane carrying our
bodies nearly disappeared above the un-living fog; the lucky lucky
of it all. I have known you through our frequent endings—the
unprotected kiss on my neck—the impossible about you; a
> summer moment in this dystopian winter.

In some lives I've thrown my fists against your cool perfection.

Michael, what does stygian mean in this future? I said that I offer
peace but I think that was a lie—in love's silver temple the priestess
washes alabaster tiles and the smell of cedar lingers in your hair—

[the truth can spoil a poem]

I am death!   I am death!

The tv is stuck on a loop//faces and more faces slide-showing
> on the screen//we don't own a tv so I'm at a friend's
house watching the news picking out outrageous shoes   *and rose
earrings!* before we sprint into the evening—just some girls vs. the
rest of the world; just some boys in violent heels. The newspaper
says we should love the bomb as an explosion outside the body

opens the heart to all others—*I feel so angry*—

beneath my mascara are the kind of spiders that keep score.

I'm the already dead boy and you love me—then the painted
figures of our fathers turning into red animals in a red light like a
bright and smokeless fire, it was frightening, the weight of the air
>like a fist on my lung—I want you to believe when I
>levitated from the grave I looked devastating; seven points
>of perfect light around my mouth, my body, holy and

bioluminescent, full of miracles like pink nail polish neat between
the lines of my flesh—*nothing messy*—white robed as a savior
saying *let my love heal your wounds* telling truths with sugar
>but

I was stained when I came back—bending around you as a stray cat
to drink water. When I turned into this animal, I slept lightly,
jumping when you sat on the bed, squeezing under the couch
for hours to avoid you

>my arms tight around my chest   near my knees.
>*I'm the boy that you love and I'm already dead.*

Can you believe I think I'm the hero?
>Can you believe I think I'm the only one?

When Jesus comes for us at last—*my final patriarch!* The party
>has ended and we have spent the evening outside of it
and this apartment and these bodies and this city—*no more
martyrs*—like the danger outside ourselves

>>dare not exist.

SECRET ENDING:

True Names Defeat Overdose

glory hole:halo:Spirit Door:moonsaint:zig-a-zig-ah::and::ziggurate:
    Ur-Crush:partykid:morethanthing:

alive alive alive:my grandma:taught me::that::and
                      stillness::interior:Unpeelment and
    possession:spoiled milk grin:camera-bang:

Beautiful:slumber

        K I S S KISS M E

the un-leaving Other:once upon a resurrection:wish-make:
andOctober:

flying in the silver voiced
skies of the gold millennium
    boots painted with holograms

        wild birds arranging themselves in constellations

        foretelling the doom of evil
        by bending time into a golden circle—
        like a lasso holding lives together
        wearing these hopes as a hooped crown and
        raiding the tombs of the dead with incantations—
            devastating death with my devotion
        each name leaving my mouth as a promise
            each name leaving my mouth as a blade
    and when the crystal broke it was not beyond remaking—

the boy in the swing
    suspended in mid-air like

    a magician's trick, glassy-
    eyed, holding a red crescent
    with my teeth—toothsome boy chewing
    moonlight—
       as collapsible

 as a star or a black hat with
 as many secret pockets
 as the truth—pull from my darkness

 as my darkness makes more for you to take,
    see how
 I am as infinite as nothing and the world
 disappears like the closing of a blind fold

 or an eyelid—I am as pale as the gloves
 you slip your hands in and

if love was not enough:love became enough in my body:
  which holds three new galaxies and several thousand
  dreams like when we kiss the dead bodies

and they rise in shapes that they choose.

MITCHELL KING is a runaway witch living in Kansas City. His work appears online and in print at BOAAT, The Adroit Journal, BadPony, Gigantic Sequins, Baest, Rust+Moth, Nat.Brut and more. He is the 2017 winner of the New South Poetry contest and holds an MFA in poetry from Stony Brook Southampton.
@star_fag

www.ingramcontent.com/pod-product-compliance
Lightning Source LLC
Chambersburg PA
CBHW030346100526
44592CB00010B/853